AF416097

First edition: February 2025
© Copyright of the work: Inés Ponce Giménez
© Copyright of the edition: Angels Fortune Publishing Group
© Copyright of the translation: Teresa Ponce Giménez

Editing by Mª Isabel Montes Ramírez
ISBN: 979-13-990030-0-0
Digital ISBN: 979-13-990030-1-7
Layout and cover design: Cristina Lamata

©Grupo Editorial Angels Fortune
www.angelsfortuneditions.com
info@angelsfortune.com

Barcelona (España)

All Rights reserved.
No part of this publication may be reproduced, distributed, or transmitted in any form or by any means, including photocopying, recording, or other electronic or mechanical methods, without the prior written permission of the publisher, except in the case of brief quotations embodied in critical reviews and certain other noncommercial uses permitted by copyright law.

TRAILS OF HOPE

Insights of a mountain woman
along the trek of caregiving

Inés Ponce Giménez

Translated by Teresa Ponce

AUTHOR'S NOTE

Writing can be healing, and it can bring you relief in times when it is difficult to see clearly. This humble collection of insights, with illustrations of my own, written in the heart of Nordic nature, has been my lifeline for the past two years. Presented as a diary, it is the result of a self-help process to go forward, with better spirits, during the very arduous journey of facing the cancer disease of my dear and beloved companion of adventures. These stories have helped me find the strength to accompany him, care for him and finally endure grief and loss.

I want to express my sincere admiration to all the people with cancer who, every day, have to walk through this difficult and uncertain route. And, of course, I sympathize with their carers, striving every second of their days to support, relieve pain and maintain the dignity of their relatives, friends or patients with so much affection and delicacy.

By purchasing this book, you can contribute a little bit to the critical challenge of cancer research and the support of all those affected.

NOTE TO THE ENGLISH VERSION

The High Aragon region is located in the Spanish side of the central Pyrenees, where mountains are higher and people are shaped by the terrain. Deep valleys and steep massifs have forged their character, their tongue and their passions. With 160 peaks rising over 3000 metres above sea level, the challenge is served.

Teresa Ponce

MOUNTAIN STRENGTH AND ENERGY

3 May 2023

For a few months now, two complicated struggles are being fought in my immediate surroundings.

The first of them, well known to all, is being carried out in High Aragon lands. From the very moment the #savecanalroya movement was created, I identified with it. Despite the physical distance that separates me, I felt closely linked, and so I joined the thousands of testimonies that are raising their voice to defend its essence. Only by keeping it free and wild will we preserve its unique environmental wealth and biodiversity.

It's a very topical issue and there's still a long way to go before this jewel of a landscape is acknowledged as the great natural park that it is. It could be the steppingstone to start a different development model in High Aragon area, this time more sustainable and actually considering the next generation. I will keep an eye on the unfolding of events, but if I am to highlight something, as a summary of this first struggle, it's the responsible, civic movement held by so many, many mountain people and mountaineers who, from the very beginning and without hesitation, have put all their Pyrenean energy to stop this madness. From the bottom of my heart, my most sincere admiration.

The second of the battles I referred to at the beginning of this article is currently being fought in a much more intimate setting: our home. The complicated and treacherous cancer disease has impacted on us. From the beginning of this whole nightmare, relatively not long ago, I started a digital movement called #mountainenergyforJorge.

Throughout more than forty days of hospital stay, we kept receiving messages and videos from family and friends sending their prayers, strength and mountain energy to my great companion of adventures. They were giving us all their support and affection, and for this we will be eternally grateful. Despite the 1500 miles that separate us from our beloved Pyrenees, the whole magnitude of that incredible power reached us in ways words can't comprehend. The cold images of the Nordic landscape surrounding us didn't concern us at all, for we had our own internal heating source. At the moment, the recovery process is proving to be slow, and the treatment challenging. Each day is a new adventure, even if it has little to do with mountains this time. We don't know what tomorrow will bring forth, but we live day by day with the strength and values that the Pyrenees have forged on us for so many years, imprinting our very DNA.

Both movements, #savecanalroya and #mountainenergyforJorge, were born almost simultaneously, two battles still being fought day after day, where you can't afford to ever lower your guard. Mountain strength and energy is the link between them, empowering its bearers with extraordinary force.

We'll keep on marching without dismay. Hold on, beloved Jorge! Stay put, dearest Canal Roya! For those who endure shall win.

THIS SUMMER

29 June 2023

Robins, white wagtails, great tits, blackbirds, thrushes. The songs and flights of these small birds take turns successively as I contemplate them from the terrace overlooking the garden. Their swift movements impel me to stay alert and not miss anything. In the same breath, I let the aromas of lilacs, magnolias, rhododendrons and wild roses numb my senses as they fill my lungs. The sound from the leaves of birches and rowans as they wave in the soft breeze soothes me, and I take delight in their calm, peaceful dances. Spectacular!

In a few weeks, redcurrants will be in season, they are beginning to ripe. Their bittersweet flavour is always related to this summer time. We will have to wait for a couple of months yet to eat the apples. Then, pies, jams and roasted apples will come to our tables. This is our way to sweeten the autumn.

Close to our home are the waters of Lake Borlången, which are lukewarm now. We've had very high temperatures during the months of May and June. Sinking into its depths at dawn is a renewing experience which activates my body and mind, encouraging me to embark on the new day with spirit. It feels unreal that I slide on my skis across these very icy waters during the chilly winter afternoons. That is the nature within my grasp this summer. A surrounding Nordic yet warm nature that embraces me daily to keep me awake, attentive to important things, anchoring me to the present moment, to here and now.

Pyrenean nature will have to wait this time. The big mountains in High Aragon aren't leaving their location. Their rushing fresh creek waters, the slow gentle flight of red kites and bearded vultures, as well as the kamikaze movements of swifts at sunset, will always be there. Beautiful edelweiss flowers, irises, gentians and primulas will keep on blooming on the slopes of those millennial massifs.

Pyrenean ascents, which have been a part of our family and friends summer adventures, are taking a break this year. Sometimes life takes a challenging turn and defies you to prove your worth, strength, and endurance. However, the values I have forged from mountain experiences throughout so many years have hardened me, providing me with the fortitude as much as the physical capacity to face any challenge.

This summer I am keeping Pyrenean nature in my memory, like etched pictures, while it's Nordic nature who embraces me and instils me with serenity and peace of mind.

SMILE

12 August 2023

I love this picture. It truly reflects my spirit. A restless spirit who enjoys challenges and of course overcoming them. In touch with nature, a wild nature in its purest form. Hiking at heights, always thinking of flying high, feeling the fresh air on my face and the sense of freedom. With a cheerful smile that reflects a brave attitude, one that could well be summed up in the way a student of mine likes to describe me: *echá p'alante* (enterprising).

Another student observed a couple of months ago, by the end of the school year, how much she had learnt after four years attending my classes. And little had to do with the subject I teach. Apparently at some point I was asked about my permanent smile and my cheerful character. She perfectly recalled my answer: I had told them about my toolbox.

Because that's what life is about for me. Every day, every stage in life, poses new challenges, as wilderness itself does. So, the secret lies in being able to use the right device to solve the different events unfolding. It isn't so much what is going on around you, but the way you handle it and to what degree you let it affect you. Sometimes life changes come without a warning. The only thing you can do with these sudden, enforced changes is to get along with them. They will take you on a rollercoaster of emotions which you will have to surf as they appear. That's when your toolbox comes in super handy. You identify the emotions and then find the most suitable tool to deal with it. What my students don't know is that the most powerful utensil kept in my magic box is being in contact with them. Everything they teach me, the powerful energy they pass on me.

A new school year begins, and I am meeting them again next week. It's been a strange summer, far from my mountains, from that wild nature that allows me to fly and get wrapped up in all its magic. The peace and quiet of the Nordic scenery surrounding me serves me as an anchor to the present moment as well as a reminder of my life purpose, giving me the chance to let go what I can't control.

A new school year begins on Thursday 17 and, just like the picture heading this writing, I smile, thumbs up, and think: 'Here we go, let's give our all!'

POSTCARDS

26 September 2023

La Gomera, Granada, Costa del Sol, Jaca, Oslo, Gothenburg, South Africa and Italy are some of the places from where I was sent postcards this year.

Receiving postcards from different parts of the world offers a taste of adventure starting from the thrilling moment you take them out of the mailbox. Every time a new postcard arrives, I begin the same ritual. I read it carefully, observing the handwriting style with affection, then I take delight in the stamp, and finally I flow with the content of the message, as if the words and sentences carried me somehow to its place of origin and I could find myself standing next to the sender. I don't feel these sensations whenever someone texts me.

Then I go to my dear wall, where I exhibit them all, and I figure out the best spot to hang it. The wall of a corridor I walk through several times a day. It's my small international mural, where pictures and drawings talk to me and whisper tales of friendship, love and affection. Their messages embrace me every day, accompanying me despite having been written thousands of miles apart and in different moments in time.

I feel happy about my little art exhibition, but mainly I'm enormously grateful to be included in the lives of a handful of people who generously saved a little free time during their travels or holydays to buy a postcard and a stamp and share a tiny corner of their lives with me.

Art and friendship melt on a magic wall with the power to take me flying around the globe. Travelling had never been so gratifying. Thank you, postcards. Thank you, dear little people.

WALK AGAINST CANCER

17 October 2023

On October 22 a walk against cancer is held in my hometown. At a modest price of ten euros you can sign up and cover the three-mile course to support this noble cause. Funds raised at the event are assigned to research aiming to mitigate this disease which is spreading across our society at a galloping rate. No matter your age, sex, financial situation, job position or social status. You don't see it coming, it suddenly shows up and settles in any family home without warning.

Many of us have a father, mother, partner, sibling or friend who's suffered from it or is going through it at the moment. They are the actual participants of their daily walk against cancer. An admirable path, full of both physical and mental strain, thoughts, waits, relapses, hopes, fears, frustrations and countless emotions, thus becoming true role models of perseverance. No one taught them at school or university to brace themselves for such a circumstance. They must learn everything as they come across difficulties along this winding road.

Some of them are lucky to leave this nightmare behind, but many are bound to the disease until the end. Oncology wards at hospitals are busy with people in treatment hoping to belong to the first group. Their looks talk on their own: why me?

Every week when I step into the ward and find many of these patients, I respectfully look at them conveying my sincere admiration. Every day, when I look my life partner in the eye, I tell him without words: "You're not alone. Come on! We will keep on together in this walk against cancer."

I SEE YOU, I FEEL YOU, I ADMIRE YOU

5 November 2023

I see you, I feel you, I smell you, I admire you...

I know that nothing stays the same, that you are going to fade. The day will come when you'll disappear, although your presence I won't ever forget.

I see you, I feel you, I smell you, I admire you...

And yet, I'm saddened by the fact of losing you. I'll have to reconcile myself with the idea of not seeing you, but all these years by your side will remind me of my great luck.

I see you, I feel you, I smell you, I admire you...

Despite everything, you're going to take flight, and I wish you the best. I know wherever you go, here or there, in this earthly world or into space, this feeling we share will remain.

You're going to fly and enjoy the journey...

But today you're here with me and I see you, I feel you, I smell you, I admire you. ❤

MÖRK

25 November 2023

The edifying trek begins. A yearly adventure, forgotten as soon as it's over. So much so that at this moment, when I find myself at the beginning of this exciting experience, I am aware that nothing will be as it was last time.

Mörk is starting, the season when days are extremely short and icy nights become exhaustingly eternal. This mesmerizing fathomless charcoal-black darkness takes hold of you from the very moment you wake up and open your eyes. Then a few hours of relief, so you can scarcely feel the timid warmth of the solar star. And finally, before you even realise, it comes back to you like a boomerang.

Despite it may, at first sight, seem an everlasting nightmare, I find in these long afternoons of Nordic retirement the opportunity to travel through reading, while I sit down by the light and heat of the fire in the hearth, and embrace the company of the calm instrumental music that warms up my soul.

In the same way, a fascinating and unique inner journey also begins. Over a background of music, a good read and the sound of crackling fire, my mind finds help to value all the experiences lived in this year that is at its tail end. A succession of gleeful and bitter events like the pages of an adventure book, my personal adventure. Chapter after chapter, I am learning to sail in this ocean of life, back and forth, a carousel, a seesaw where I try to maintain balance. A balance that is paramount to attain my most intimate peace and quiet.

Wellcome, *mörk*! May the adventure begin!

PLAYING IN THE SNOW

20 January 2024

Snow is cold poetry. Like a mantle of white purity, it drenches the soil and transforms the landscape, silently and peacefully, bearing a touch of hope until the arrival of all the colours and sounds of spring.

During the hard months of winter, snow fills me with optimism, for it lights up the dark eternal nights of this time of the year, magnifying the sun beams or reflecting the moonlight.

Snow is synonymous with peace, calm and tranquillity. Soft snowfalls with their flakes floating down weightless pose an invitation to retreat, reading and contemplation. Sounds are muffled in the snow as silence lies around your shoulders guiding you to muse, listen to your inner voice and move forward into uncharted territories.

At the same time, this white layer induces to engage in games, laughter and fun. The kids bustle in the playground is astonishing these weeks. The happy faces of children sliding down the hill in a sleigh or skating on the improvised ice rink of a frozen football pitch says it all. No below-zero temperature can stop the drive and energy kids in these early ages are brimming with.

The enjoyment is not for children alone. In the second half of my life I keep embracing the opportunities the new day brings. Given a window of good weather, I don't hesitate, I put on my Nordic skis. Then I glide down the slope and after that, not without effort, I push myself along the streets of the small Nordic town where I live. On the frozen lake under a thick layer of snow, I can also feel that sense of freedom. This open space, surrounded by wild nature, allows me to go forward with my skis at top speed. Each moment is different.

However, snow entails some risks that you can't ignore. One would think that fatal accidents occur in high mountains, under freezing temperatures and extremely adverse conditions, but reality has stricken us this week to remind us not to let our guard down. In a snowy playground, an unexpected misfortune has taken the life of a seven-year-old young neighbour, and it has shrunk our hearts.

Turned into a white shroud this time, snow has made me feel a profound, immense sadness and has reminded me to always approach it with the great respect it deserves. Rest in peace, little one, walk now in the land of life.

DAILY LIFE

26 January 2024

I love daily life. On any given day, you get up early and, after washing yourself, slowly head for the kitchen. There you prepare a simple breakfast and sit intending to enjoy that brief moment. Your loyal friend follows you and sits at your feet, hoping for a lucky share. It smells of coffee and toast, and silence wraps your shoulders like a warm cardigan.

Trapped in your thoughts, you look at the window and sense it must be cold outside. A sip of hot coffee reminds you how lucky you are. You refuse to turn the radio on, whishing that magical, private and intimate moment belonging to you won't die out. You don't want the metallic voice to wake you up, bringing you back to reality.

A new sip from your smoking mug takes you to different times, different places, different emotions, but you come back soon enough. You can still feel in your hands the heat from the pottery and look through the window again. You are here and the time is now. Don't let nostalgia paralyse you.

A bite of your moist toast with rubbed tomato, oil and salt takes you to your immediate duties, your musts. An odd feeling sinks in. But it's so cozy in here. You just want to stay a little longer, here, now. Yet, a glance at the clock and you know it. You have to get started. The complex mechanism of the workday begins, and you let it guide you. So you finish your simple yet succulent delicacy and clean everything behind you.

Before switching off the light, you look again at that magic corner in your home and think: "It will happen again tomorrow." Oh, how I love daily life!

TOGETHER TO THE LAST SUMMIT

24 August 2024

What are you doing for the next sixty years?

You asked me this question on a September day in 1996. Since then, twenty-eight years have passed, and many have been the thrilling adventures we have lived together.

We have raised two wonderful daughters and a wonderful son. They have grown up in a loving home, in contact with nature, sport, culture and music. All these elements have endowed them with great sensitivity, strength of spirit and, especially, with infinite kindness. All three of them are beautiful goodhearted people. We didn't do it that bad, did we?

We have climbed together many summits in our beloved Pyrenees, some in the Alps and the highest in the Atlas range, in Africa. Mountaineering has been the activity which has bonded us together as a couple, nurtured our family love with high doses of strength, courage and determination in adversity. Many have been the mountain metaphors we have used to describe our relationship and our family life. We met in this environment, and it's been our allied ever since.

This love of rocky heights also launched you out to both the American and Asian continents, where you actually fulfilled your teenage dream, built after attending in Zaragoza a talk with the world-famous alpinist Peter Haveler. You have always described walking through the Himalaya surrounded by those eight-thousand-metre peaks as "beyond overwhelming." You reached Camp 2 at seven thousand metres, but the summit wasn't the goal at that time. Your priority was to take care, as the expedition doctor, of your Civil Guard companions. So well you did it that the experience was a resounding success.

In fact, your vocation to help others, to take care and ease the pain of other people has been constantly present in your life, be it domestic or professional. You have been held in high regard in every hospital and health centre where you have worked as a doctor. Also a pioneer career-wise, you were one of the first doctors assigned to the new hospital built in Jaca when it opened doors in 1989. And when medical mountain rescue was set up in Aragon, there you were, at the starting line so no one had to tell you a thing or two about it. Eternal contributor to the Red Cross, varying from first aid trainer to a president position during your last period in Jaca. Always guided by your vocation for service, you didn't fail to attend local sport events featuring an EMS ambulance.

This vocation was precisely your reason to embark on a new adventure, from our most beloved Jaca to the furthest away place in Europe, to settle our residence in the Swedish region of Småland. A lack of doctors in these latitudes allowed you to pursue new professional challenges while offering our children an opportunity to expand their minds, to get in touch with another culture and another way of thinking, proceeding and being in the world.

And here we are today, on your sixty-third birthday, almost three decades after you asked me that question. Like I said, we have set off for heart-pounding adventures many times throughout all these years, but certainly none as hard and difficult as the one we are living now. Cancer disease is consuming you. The weakness and immunosuppression derived from this disease have taken you down a very complicated and painful road. You are so weary that you just want to stop suffering, be calm and at peace. Once again, as I always have, I walk with you. We keep doing it together, with strength, courage and determination in adversity. I offer you the only thing I have, all my love. You are not alone, and with this simple rucksack we continue advancing towards the last summit. ILY.

PRESENCE

18 September 2024

A feeling of sadness spreads everywhere these days. My heart is so shrunken I can't scarcely feel its beat. An immense void suffocates me since you left, and I struggle to find anything to fill it. I figure all these sensations will grow a little bit dimmer every day, time will pass relentlessly, and slowly I will manage to pull myself together. Nevertheless, amid this pandemonium of turbulent feelings, I'm sensing something that, for now, is proving difficult to describe. It's happened at moments imbued with infinite calmness.

Some days ago I woke up quite early, and as I drew the curtains I saw a fawn through the window, grazing peacefully in the garden. Unexpectedly it raised its head, and we gazed at each other. It only lasted a few seconds, but that clean, transparent innocence gave me great peace of mind.

I often go out in the garden to hang out the washing, but for some days now, when I'm doing this simple chore, I'm surrounded by white butterflies flitting playfully in a hectic, uncontrolled pattern. Strange as it seems, this harmless game of forest fairies embraces me warmly and comforts me.

Commuting to work along winding roads through forests and lakes, I can see the red kite's majestic flight, whose shadow cast in my way seems to escort me. What I feel then is an energetic transfusion of strength and courage to keep moving forward in the midst of adversity.

In all these brief and simple moments—in the calm gaze of the fawn, in the warm embrace of the butterflies or in the magnetism of the flight of a red kite—I feel an undefined peace drawing a very comforting smile on my face. And that's when I can't help thinking that, during those countless seconds, you are with me. The force of nature heals me, moderates my pain, and I feel you very close to me. Thus, I understand that your absence is only physical. Your body is gone, but your essence, your aura, remains by my side and so it will be forever.

LETTER TO JORGE

2 November 2024

Well, Jorge, you asked me to dance a jota at your funeral and so I did. And, to be honest, it wasn't such a poor performance, after so many years without playing the castanets.

But this wish of yours wouldn't have been possible to fulfil without the invaluable help of the Alto Aragón Folk Group and some family members. So much generosity!

Difficult winds blow, I feel sad and melancholic about your departure, but at the same time I'm grateful for having known you and counted you as my dance partner for so long.

For life is like a dance. Sometimes you turn right, sometimes you turn left. There are moments when you speed up the rhythm, and moments when you slow it down.

And so the years pass. Our dance has been intensive. Along these close to three decades, we have lived everything we have dared to, not without fear or concern, but always with strength and determination in the face of adversity, the very values learnt from the mountains, our great allies.

So many things we have learnt in this great adventure, which undoubtedly has been watered with high sense of humour, mountains of laughter, but mainly with intense love. Our three wonderful children—Santi, Paula & Cris—have showed us in numerous occasions which path to follow, and, even if it was the longest or the stoniest, we would take it with confidence to spend more time with them, smoothen our dissonances and keep improving our ability to guide them. The teachings of our beloved and faithful friend Rufo have been equally valid, tempering our patience and humility until his last days.

Today marks the end of a cycle. I am dressed just as the day I started it, that February 22, 1997, in the church of Sinués. Many of those who are with us today, family and friends, were also then. Some have travelled with us along this journey, whether completely or just during some stages, and shared the good moments and those not so good. What a precious treasure! How fortunate we have been, Jorge!

Yet the circle that is being closed today is but a change of paragraph. Every experience, positive and not so positive, every lesson and flick of wisdom acquired, all the laughs and all the love and affection so keenly felt are kept safe and sound in our rucksack.

There will be more mountain ascents, feeling the cool breeze on our faces, being warmed up by powerful sunbeams, delighted with every little sound of nature and surrounded by the variety of fragrances that enraptures us as we awaken our senses... And in all these moments, your legacy, most dear and beloved Jorge, will always walk with us.

I bid you farewell with the poem Remember *Me*, by David Harkins, which you liked so much.

You can shed tears that he is gone
or you can smile because he has lived.

You can close your eyes
and pray that he'll come back
or you can open your eyes
and see all that he's left.

Your heart can be empty
because you can't see him
or you can be full
of the love that you shared.

You can cry and close your mind,
be empty and turn your back
or you can do what he'd want:
smile, open your eyes, love and go on.

Thank you for reading new literary talent.
I hope you enjoyed the read.

Feel free to visit our Bookstore
https://angelsfortune.com/

Follow us on our social networks to stay informed.

Isabel Montes
Writer and founding publisher of
Angels Fortune Publishing Group

www.ingramcontent.com/pod-product-compliance
Lightning Source LLC
Chambersburg PA
CBHW031808150726
47989CB00006B/2930